LO-PAN

SUBTLE

ALR022

Published by

Aqualamb

LO-PAN
Jesse Bartz - Drums
Jeff Martin - Vocals
Chris Thompson - Guitars
Skot Thompson - Bass

Produced, Engineered and Mixed by James Brown
Mastered by Ted Jensen at Sterling Sound
Additional Engineering by James Yost

Recorded at Reservoir Studios, NY & The Union, NY
Mixed at the The Union NY

Tape Manipulations by Rafael Anton Irisarri

All songs written and performed by LO-PAN

Cover art and book design by Eric Palmerlee for Aqualamb
Photography by:
Keith Marlowe pgs 26-27, 62-63, 68, 86, 122-123
Chris Thomspon pgs 50-51, 74-75, 98-99, 110-111
Skot Thompson pgs 14-15
Dana Sze pgs 38-39

NORTH AMERICA
Booking
Aaron Gray at Heavy Talent

Public Relations
Carl Schultz at Action! PR

EUROPE
Booking
Matthias Vandeven at Sound of Liberation

Public Relations
Mona Miluski at All Noir PR

aqualamb.org

CONTENTS

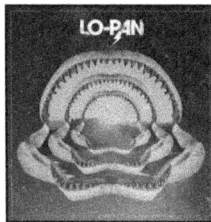

The music for *Subtle*
can be downloaded
via the link below:

http://aqualamb.org/022

01
TEN
DAYS
(3:18)

Fig. 1 House cats (Felis catus)

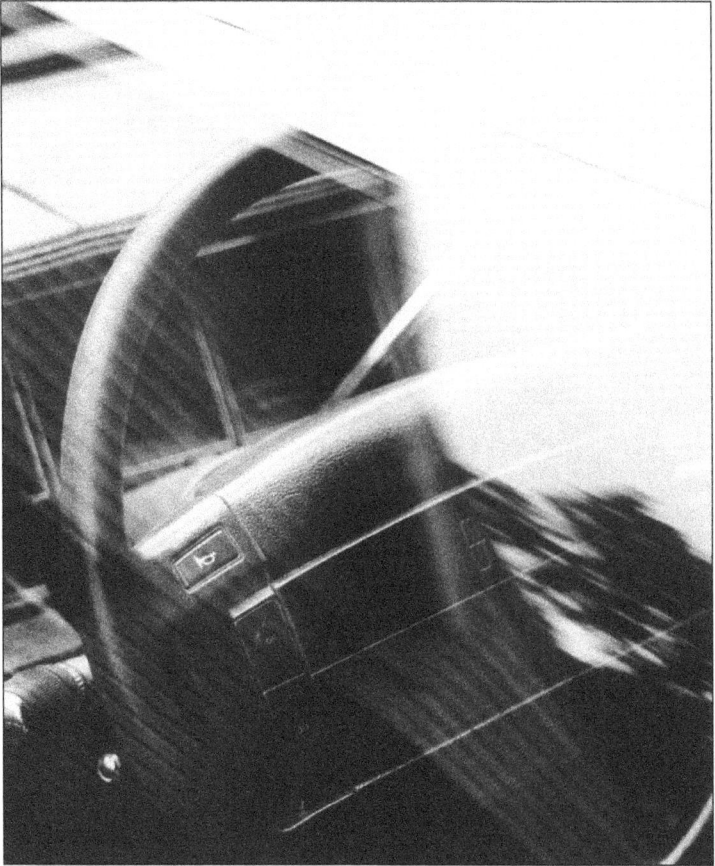

Fig. 2 Always on the move we don't break stride

Ten Days

1 10 Days 10 nights pushed all inside. One true believer. Fight all day but you never even thought to run.

2 Always on the move we don't break stride. One true believer. Run all day but you never even loaded the gun.

⚠️ I've seen you walkin around with the pieces of the things you say. I see loaded for bear.

Fig. 3   I see you winning me over

Fig. 4 I'm where I wanna be

3 Been across the saddle been across the sea. I feel so dead inside don't even think of resurrecting me.

4 Just keep on selling the dream as a means of aristocracy. I won't be fooled again. I'm where I wanna be.

5 I see the way you're pushing through. One sad deceiver. Wish for the way it was never ever meant to be. I'm not receiving your message. Stop fucking me over.

6 Broken receiver. Not believing the way you lust for disease.

Fig. 5   Been across the saddle been across the sea

7 I've seen you marching around with the pieces of the games you play.

8 I see loaded for bear. You see it's taking me over.

9 Been across the saddle been across the sea. I feel so dead inside cause of the way you're disrespecting me.

10 Just keep on selling the dream as a means of aristocracy.

11 I won't get fooled again. This is where I wanna be.

Fig. 6   I won't get fooled again

⚠️ 10 Days inside. Won't break my stride. Staying on the inside. Won't break my stride.

Fig. 7 Thorn of the Cross (Colletia Paradoxa)

Fig. 8 Various reciprocating saws

02
SAVAGE
HEART

(3:48)

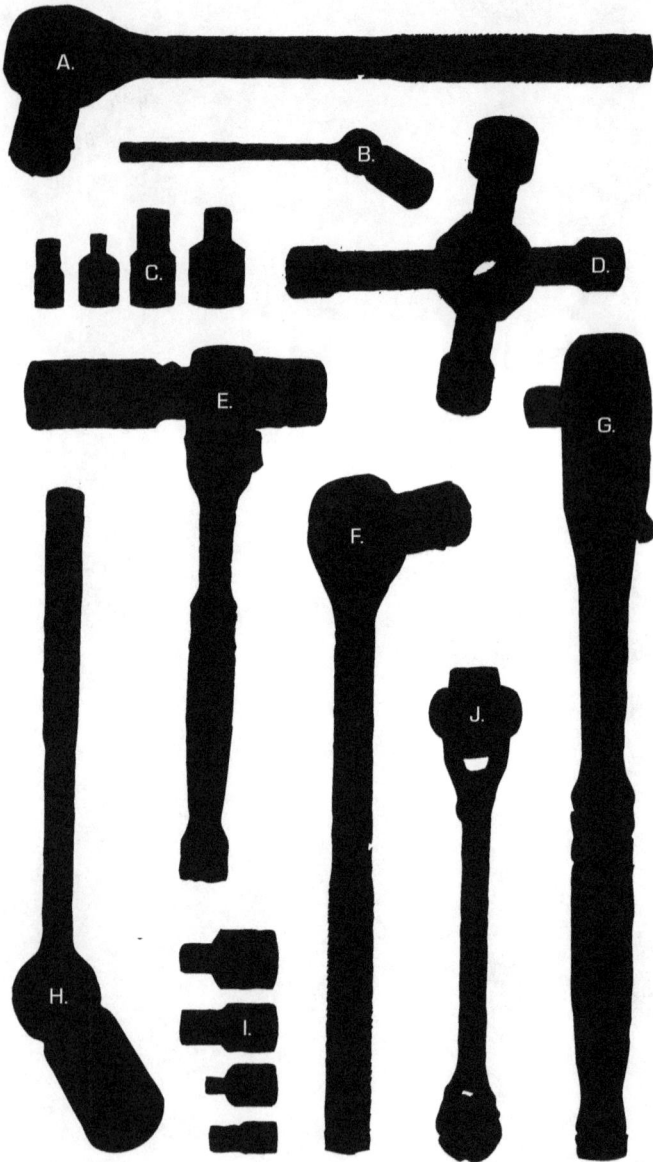

Fig. 1 Socket wrenches

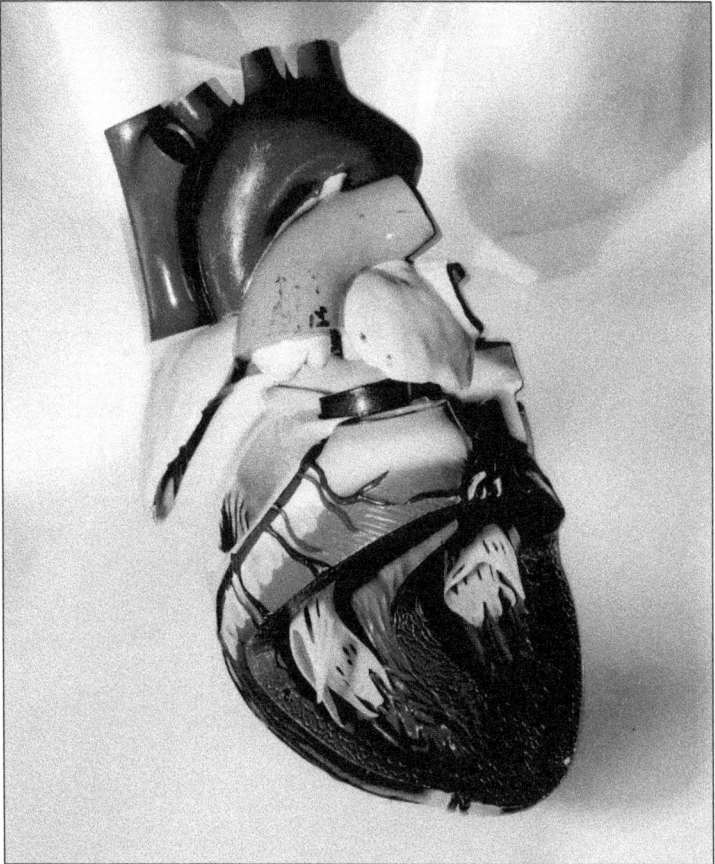

Fig. 2   Anatomical heart

Savage Heart

1 Living all alone with a Savage Heart, but every night it bleeds for you. I'll never be the one who lays it all on the line but you love me too.

2 I don't hide it well. You see right though me. Sitting in my cell. I don't control me.

3 Far from home in-side you never even crossed my mind.

Fig. 3 Shallow drownings bind

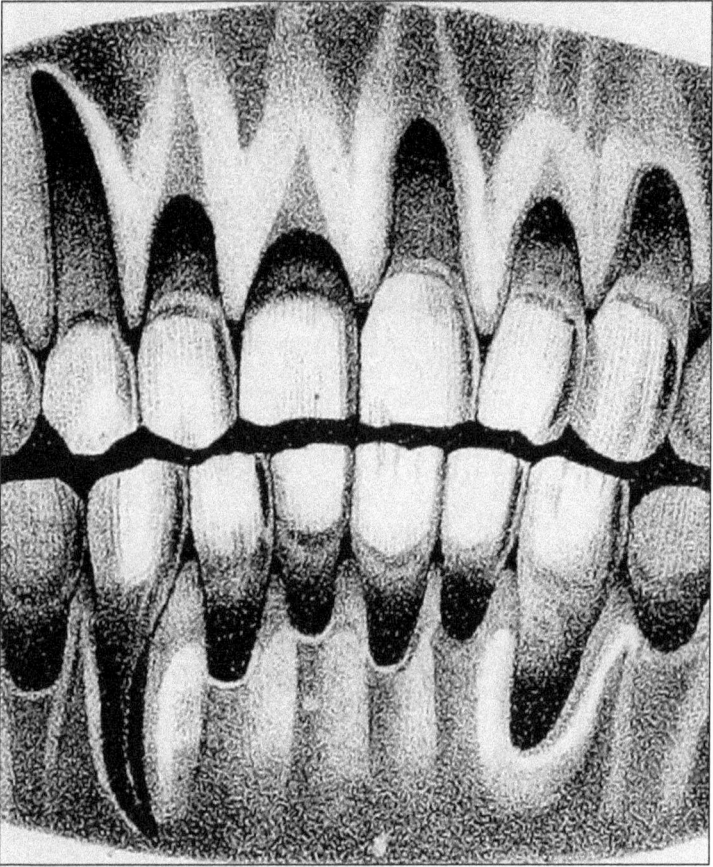

Fig. 4 Teeth is what you show

5 Riding on for miles. And tell me where you go? Hiding eye but teeth-teeth is what you show.

6 I found out to live is bittersweet. I found out my life, life was incomplete.

7 Never found a god fit to believe. Wear your Savage Heart right on your sleeve. Right on your sleeve.

Fig. 5 Shark teeth

⚠️ You said all you want you want for free. Anything in life can be yours for a fee.

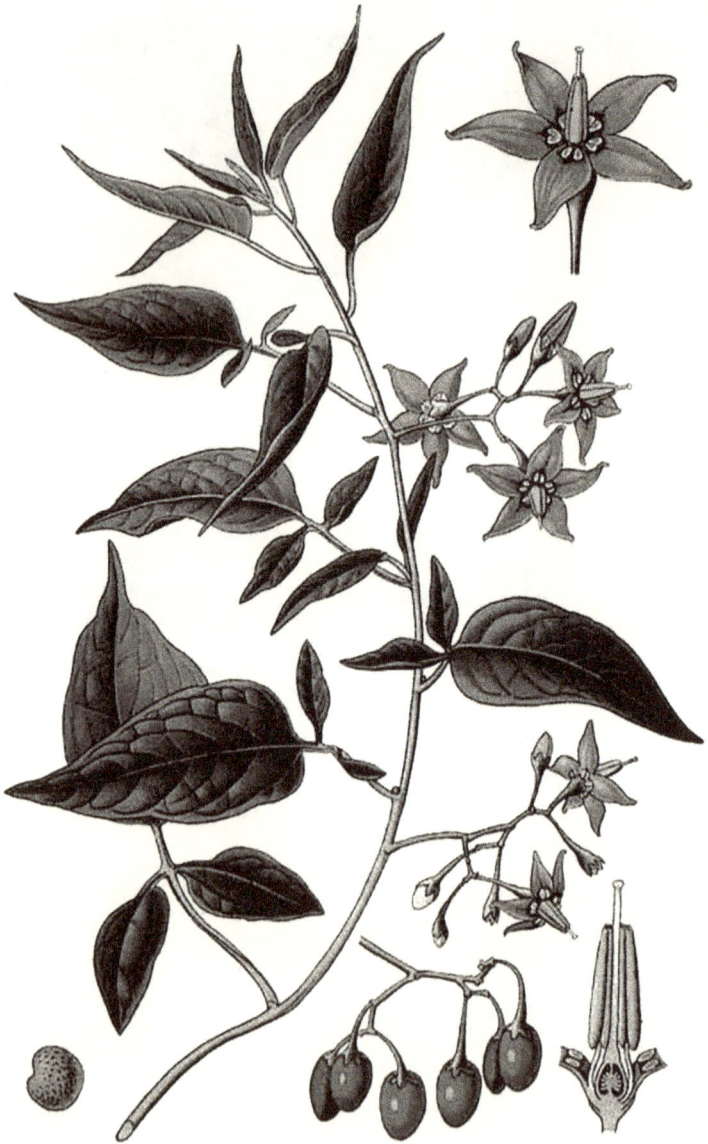

Fig. 6   Bittersweet (solanum dulcamara)

Fig. 7   You never even crossed my mind

8 Living all alone with a Savage Heart but every night it bleeds for you.

9 I'll never be the one who lays it all on the line but you love me too.

03

ASCENSION DAY

(3:36)

Fig. 1 The grandeur of water

Fig. 2 Deep blue endless ocean

Ascension Day

1 Falling down this day. Can't stand to live this way. Run without delay. **2** Hey. Could you stand to be ok? All this to say. Thoughts awash in grey. My Ascension Day. **3** Ego's on display. Pride is so passé. My Ascension Day.

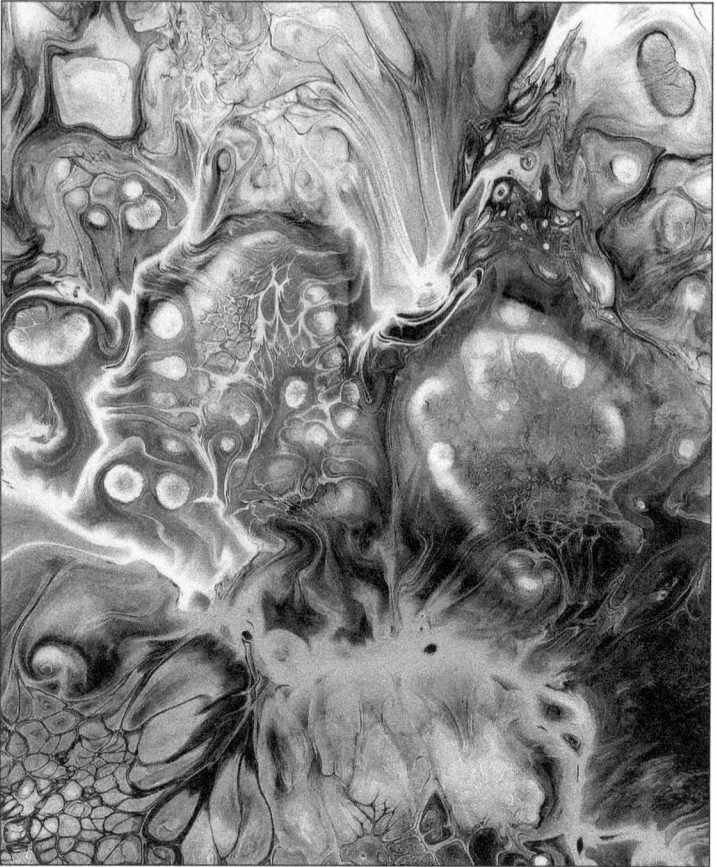

Fig. 3   Ego death

> ⚠ Live
> without
> delay.

Fig. 4   The wrath of god

4 It's all a chance to move. Another chance to feel. And live this way. **5** I've walked all alone. Even with my friends. **6** I've been upside-down and falling. But could not descend. **7** And sometimes the silence can sound so right. And the years pass so slow. On my own here late at night. I need to let it go.

Fig. 5   The silence can sound so right

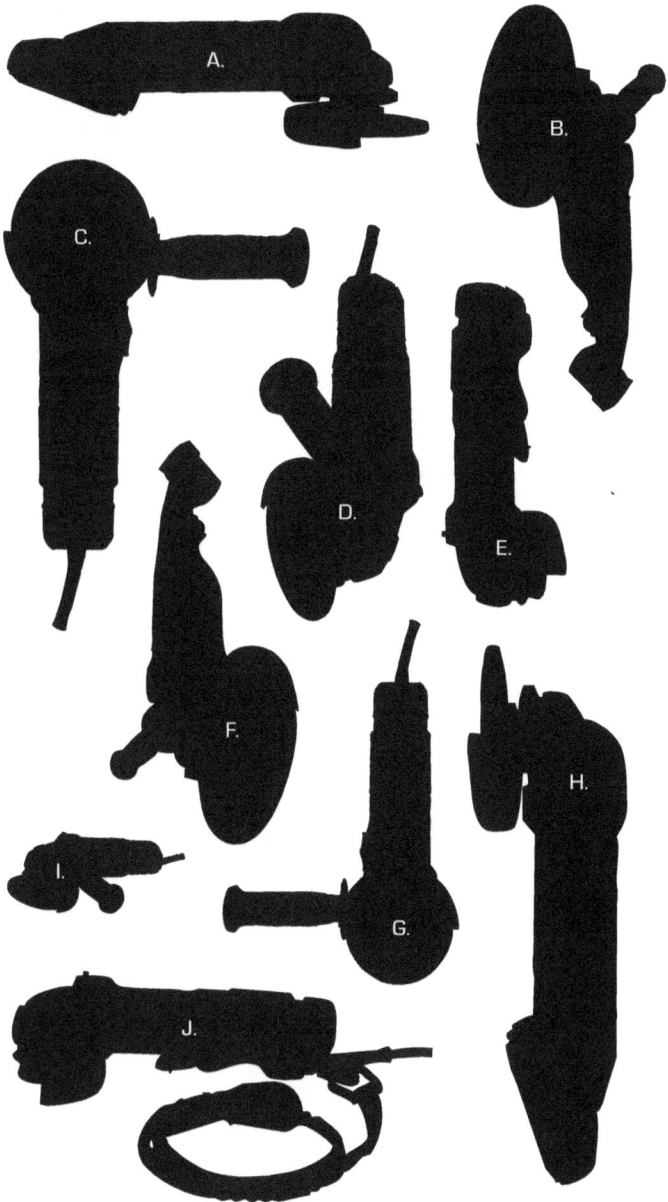

Fig. 6 An assortment of angle grinders

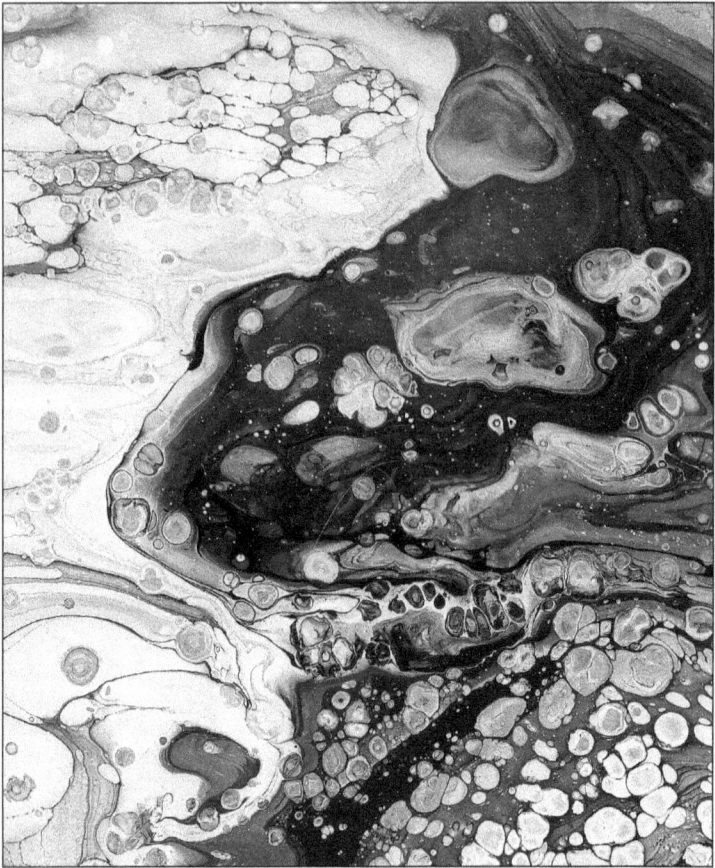

Fig. 7   Ego death pt2

⚠ When my ego's on display.
Thoughts awash in grey.
My Ascension Day.

Fig. 8   Stargazer Lily (lilium orientalis)

04
SAGE

[3:47]

Fig. 1. Babylonian artifact

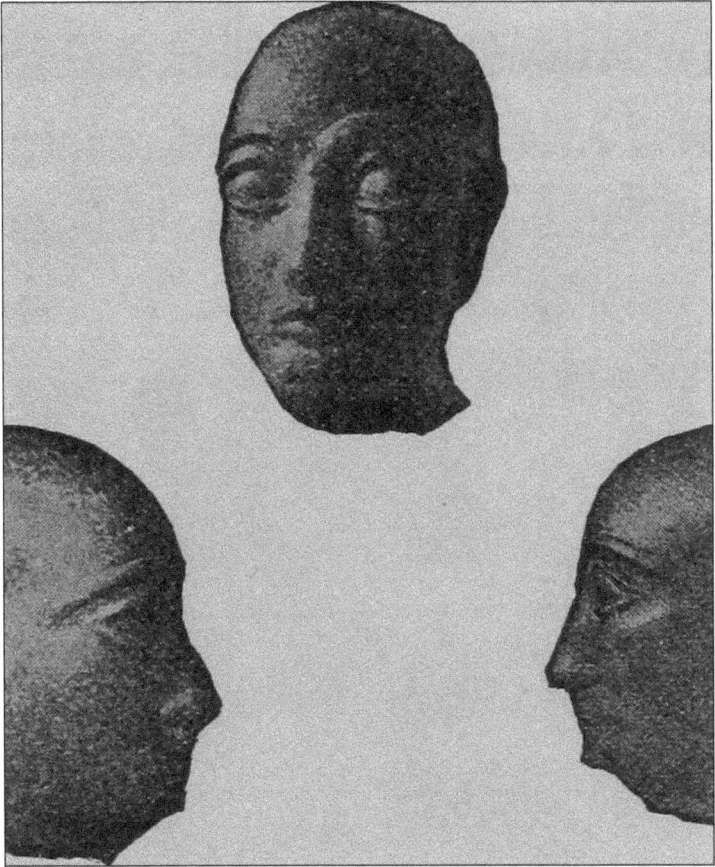

Fig. 2 Babylonian carved head

Sage

1 Long past the liar's choice I made. Sold to a lover's fate parade. Words in the darkness entertained. Lord of the lion's son profaned.

2 I am recalcitrantly Sage. It puts all heaven in a rage. Living in the golden age.

3 I never learned nothing with my feet upon the ground. Another man offering his. heart up to the crown. I never learned nothin even the truths I found.

Fig. 3   Adder skin detail

4 Hidden like the adder. Careful of the crimson rose. Open eyes are better. Much better than the path I chose.
5 I never learned nothing with my feet on solid ground. I never learned nothin even with the truths I found.
6 Hidden like the adder. Careful of the crimson rose. Open eyes are better. Much better than the path I chose.
7 I am sufficiently enraged. So tie me up and put me in a cage. I am recalcitrantly Sage. It puts all of heaven in a rage. I'm living in the golden age.

Fig. 4 Adder illustration

Fig. 5 Power drills

Fig. 6 Bits

Fig. 7 Common sage (salvia officinalis)

Fig. 8   Rose stem

8 Coiled like the adder.
Bloody from the crim-
son rose. Could have
been better. Much bet-
ter than the path I chose.

9 Careful of the adder.
Careful of the crimson
rose. Could have been
better. Much better I
suppose.

05
EVERYTHING BURNS
(6:57)

Fig. 1 Bonfire

Fig. 2 Benjamins burning

Everything Burns

1 You just sleep in the fire. You like the way it burns.
2 You never see it coming. From way behind the curve. I can't sleep in the summer. I need the bridges to burn.
3 Cause I see another storm. You better watch what you say. Assume a horrible form. I'm gonna push you away.

Fig. 3 On the edge

4 Understand now ain't the way it's supposed to be. You don't see me crying. Understand now it's the bitterness in me. What's underlying.

5 Standing on the edge of angry bitter sea. Real- izing that there ain't no guarantees. Under- stand now ain't the way its supposed to be.

6 'Cause you never see it coming. From way be- hind the curve. I can't sleep in the summer. I need bridges to burn.

7 'Cause I see another storm. You better watch what you say. Assume a horrible form. I'm gon- na push you away.

8 'Cause I'm going far away. Far from the cavity.

Fig. 4   Iceberg subsurface mass

Fig. 5　You like the way it burns

Fig. 6 Assorted hammers

Fig. 6 Forest after a wildfire

9 I'm moving far away. Far from civility. I been holding on.

10 Suffering silently 'Cause I'm blown away. Bored with ability.

11 I see another storm. You better watch what you say. Assume a horrible form. I'm gonna push you away.

12 Understand now ain't the way it's supposed to be. You don't see me crying Understand now it's the bitterness in me.

13 You don't see me crying.

Fig. 7 Baker's globe mallow (illiamna bakeri)

06
OLD NEWS/
NEW FIRE
(3:41)

Fig. 1 Skot's amp

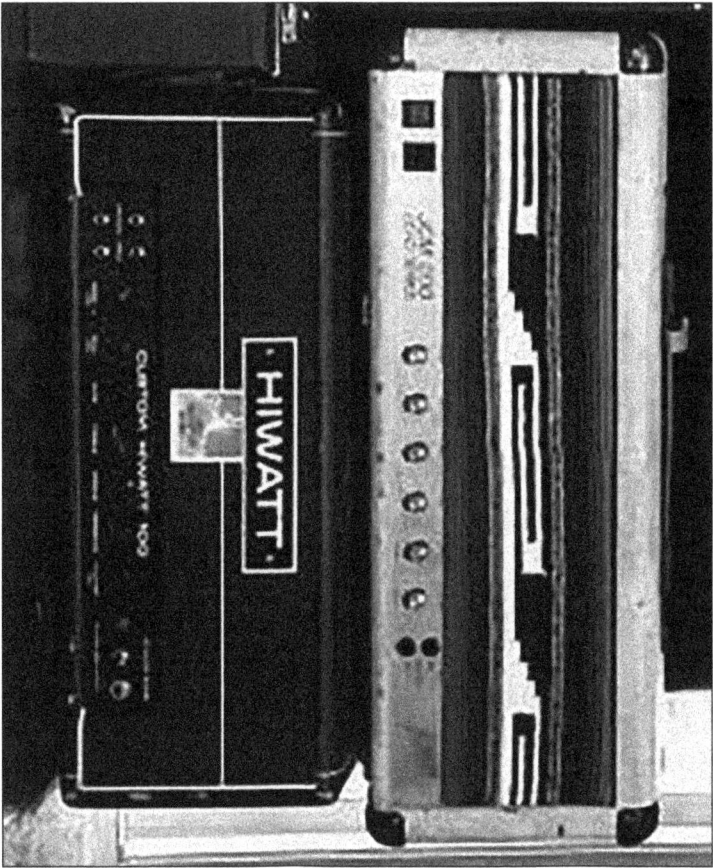

Fig. 2 ALZ's JMC800 and HIWATT

Old News/New Fire

1 Old News resurrect-
ed. I heard the wind
calling out your name.
New Fire directed. I
saw the wind circling
the flame.

2 But knowing the bur-
den I endure. I'm lost
and found in the ob-
scure.

3 Herald of dawn. Blood
in my veins is drawn. So
go out and know. The life
through the window.

Fig. 3 Chris in the studio

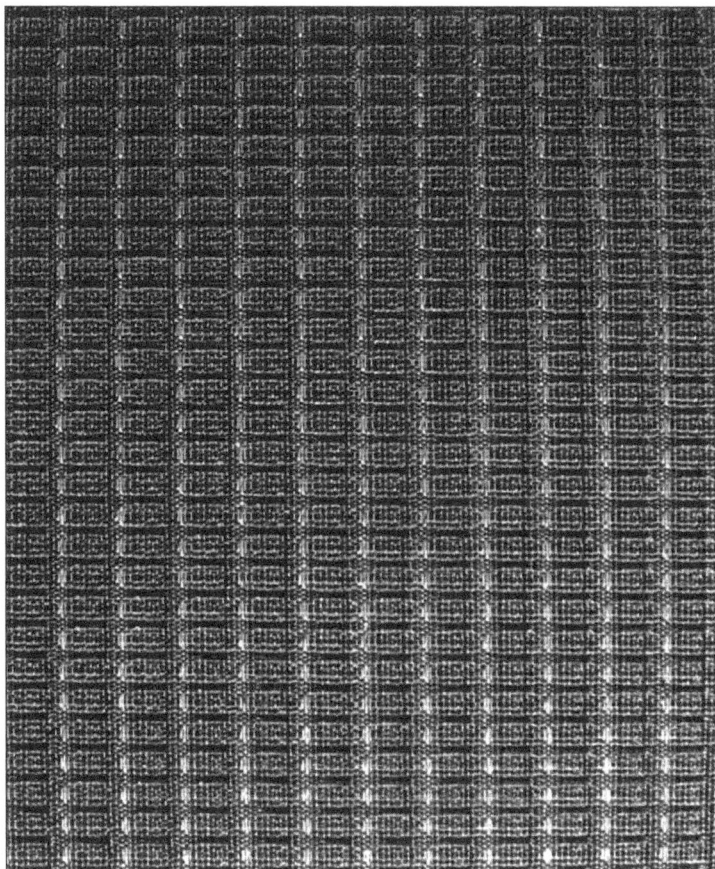

Fig. 4 Cabinet grill cloth

I'm lost and
found in the
obscure.

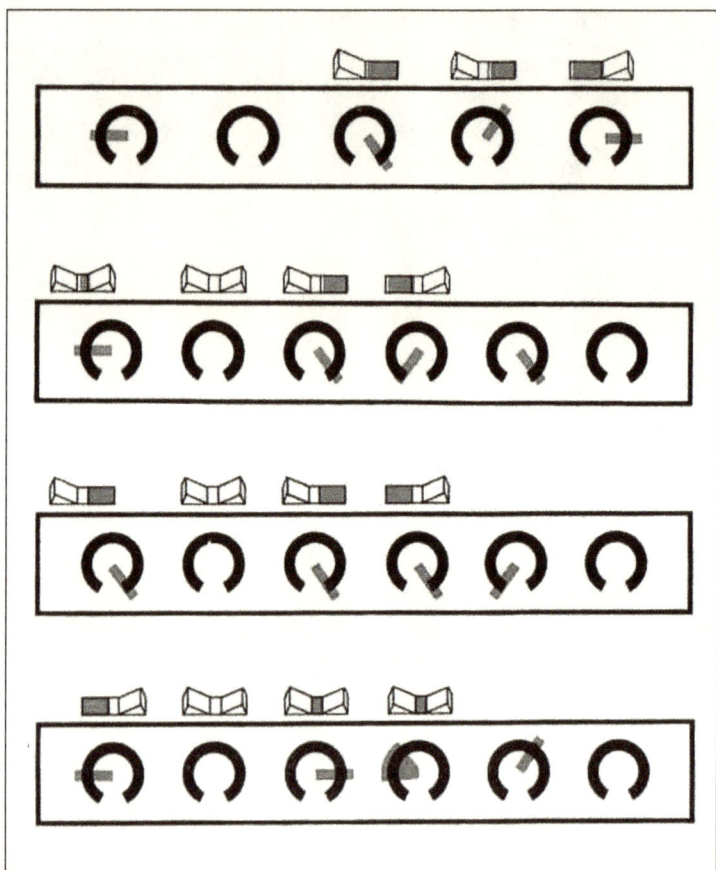

Fig. 5 Tone settings

4 Old wounds resurrect-
ed. I know your name.
I've known it from the
start. New soul respect-
ed. It always has. It'll always break my heart.
5 Still knowing the bur-
den I endure. I said I'm
lost and found in the ob-
scure.
6 Herald of dawn. Blood
in my veins is drawn.
So go out and know.
The light through the
window.
7 Bear witness to the
blood in my veins. The
product of my passage
and pain.
8 Wide-eyed behind the
window's clear pane.
Forever change affect-
ed and stained.

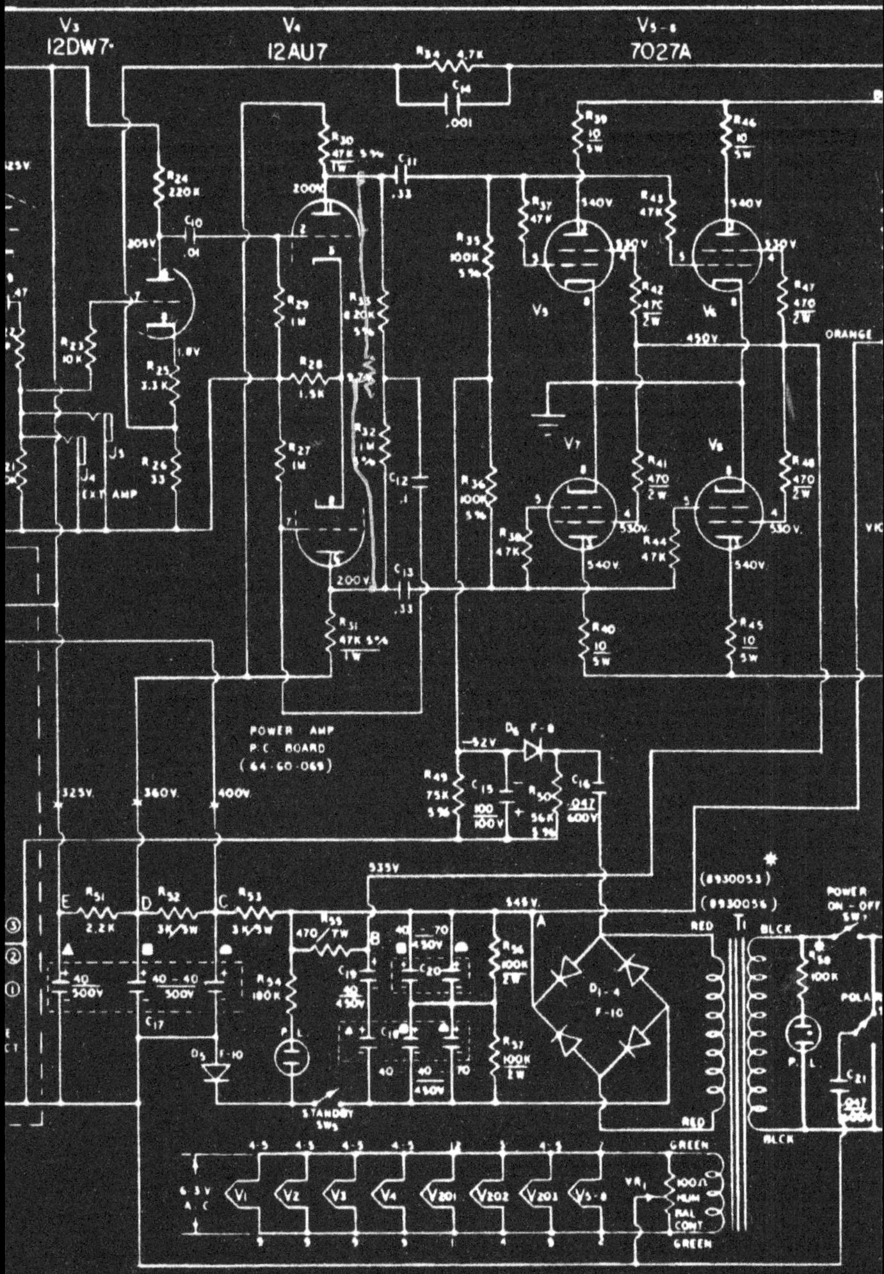

Fig. 6   Amplifier schematic

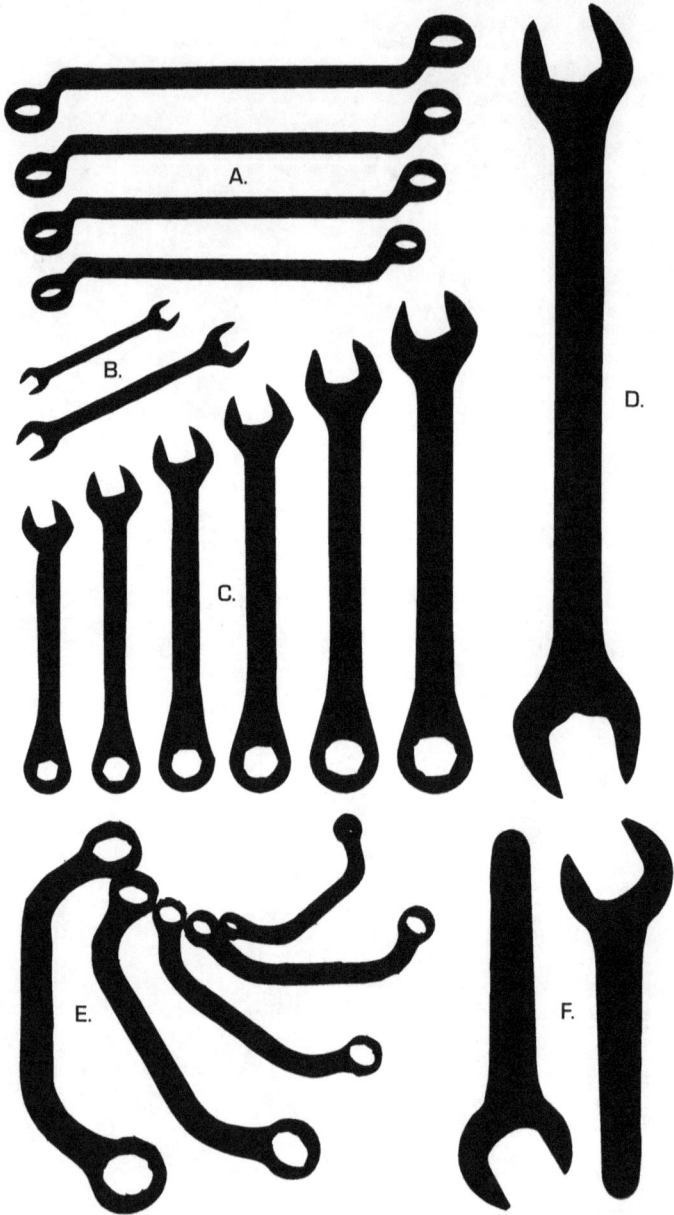

Fig. 5 Various wrenches

Fig. 7 Dahlia

07

BRING ME
A WAR

(2:58)

Fig. 1 Antifa protester

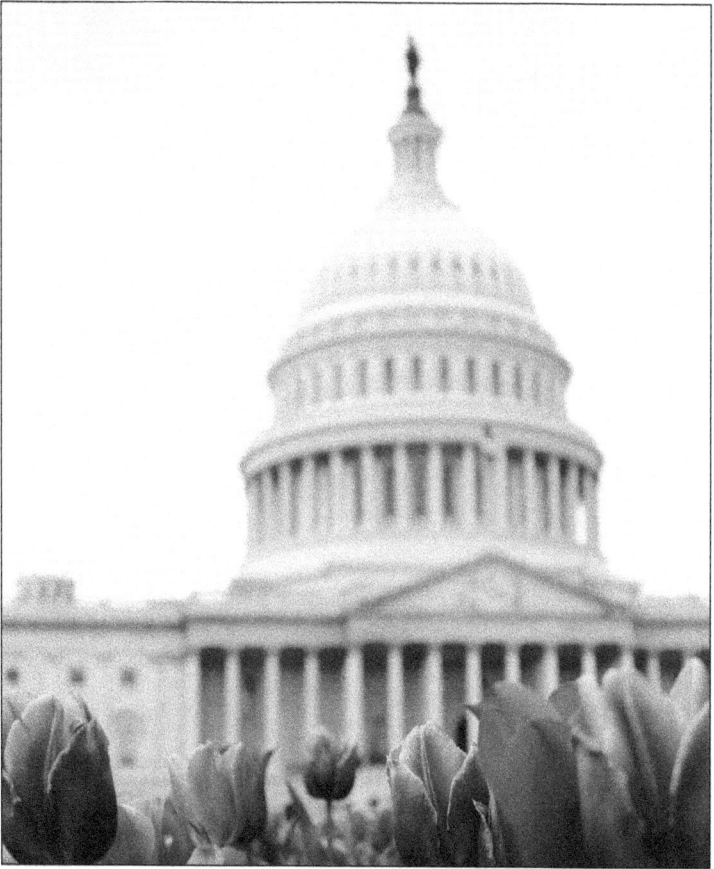

Fig. 2 U.S. Capitol Building

Bring Me A War

1 War for your mind. And I'm creeping. I'm begging and hoping to stray. No hope for the future. It's burning. It's burning away.
2 So cry havoc by moonlight. Wage War in the street.
3 I hear the drums of War. What are you waiting for? Shed blood by dark of night. Set every house alight.

Fig. 3 Wage war in the streets

Fig. 4 Blood on the streets is a warning

4 There's blood on the flowers at morning. And you know there's blood on the snow. Blood on the streets is a warning.

The blood is starting to flow. To flow!
5 So cry havoc by moonlight. Wage War in the street.

6 I hear the drums of War. What are you waiting for? Shed blood by dark of night. Set every house alight.

Fig. 5   What are you waiting for?

⚠ No hope for the future.
It's burning. It's burning
away.

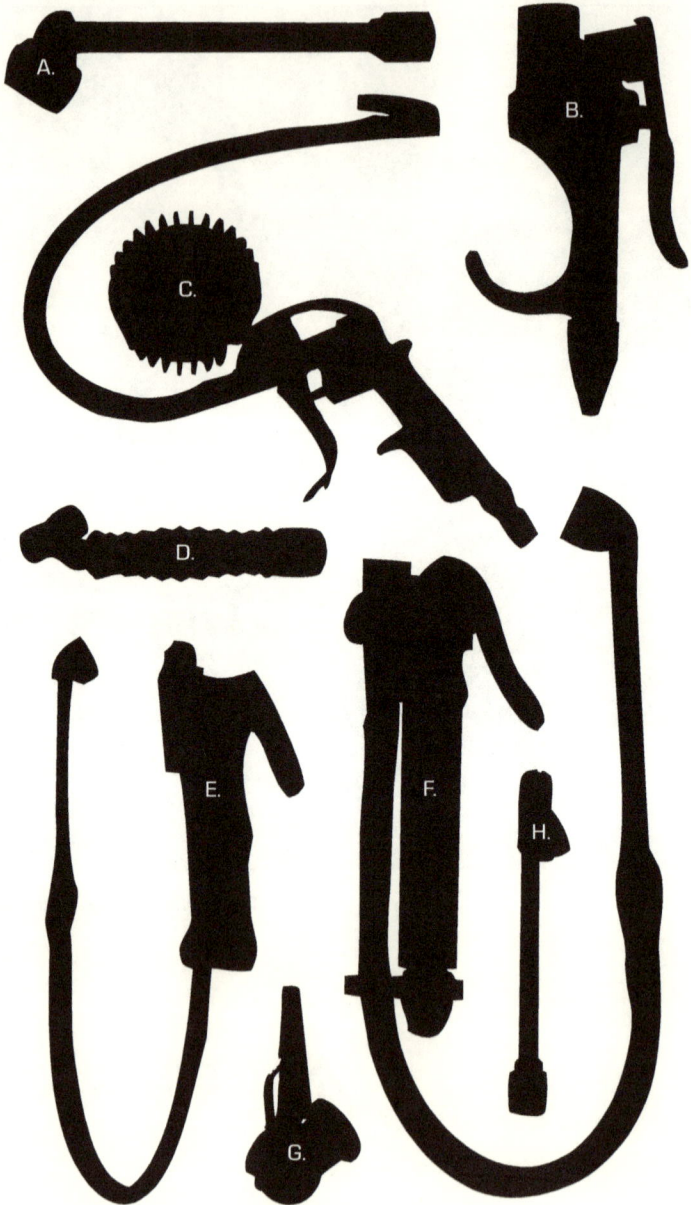

Fig. 5 Air chucks

Fig. 7   Blood Flower (asclepias curassavica)

Fig. 1   On the highway

Fig. 2   You're going to find out

A Thousand Miles

1 Oh I feel it coming on. One Thousand Miles like to take my agency. It never rains in southern California. So they say. It never feels the same once you're on that highway.

2 The Color of a dream half remembered. It's never what it seems. So take that moment and leave it where it lay. You're gonna find out. Gonna find out someday.

Fig. 3 Rivers rush

3 Oh the mountains call to me. One thousand rivers rush to cure my vacancy. The Western sky can fix whatever ails me. So I'm told. I've seen the power of the ocean. All its wonders to behold.

4 The Color of a dream half remembered. It's never what it seems. So take that moment and leave it where it lay.

You're gonna find out. Gonna find out someday. **5** I still remember. Though light is gone. Each pale September. The light at dawn.

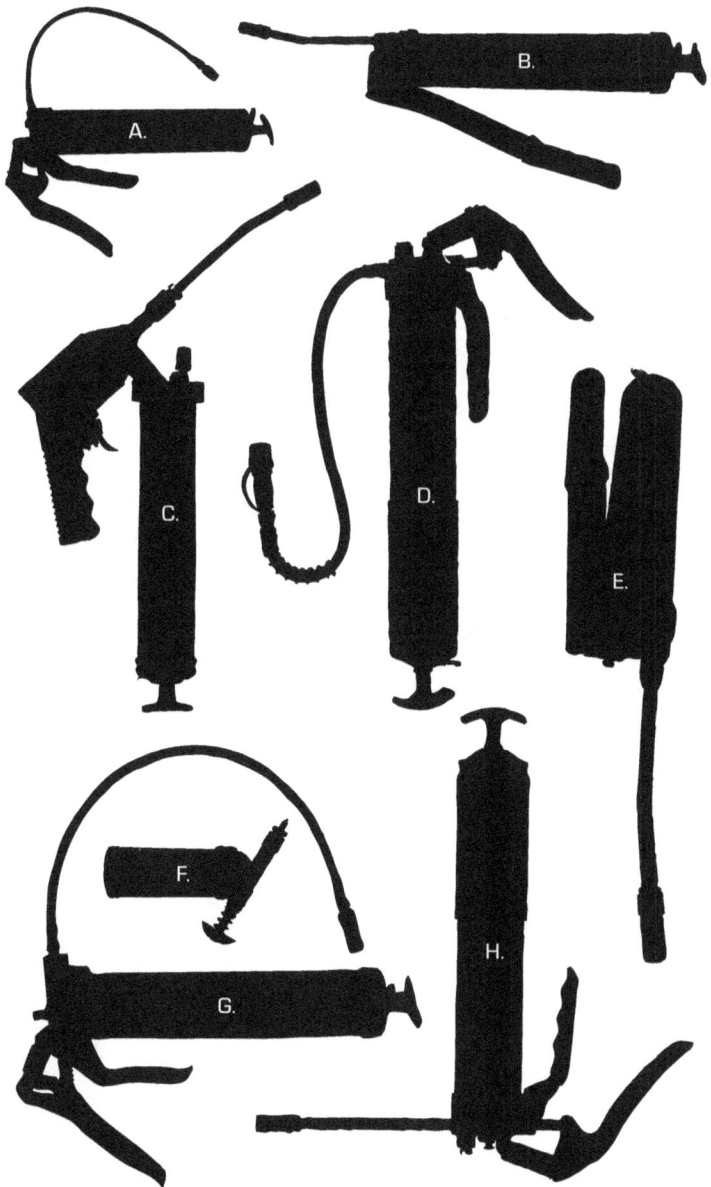

Fig. 4 Grease Guns

Fig. 5   Giant sequoia

Fig. 6 The mountains call to me

6 I lost myself in lights. Laid awake a thousand nights. Disfunction fuels my spite. Wouldn't miss a thousand nights.
7 The Color of a dream.

Half remembered. It's never what it seems. So take that moment and leave it where it lay. You're gonna find out. Gonna find out someday.

Fig. 7 California poppy (eschscholtzia californica)

09
KAHN!

(4:35)

Fig. 1 Roman theater at Pompeii

Fig. 2 Scythe

Kahn!

1 You stopped loving the skin your in. And found your path to forgiveness.
2 I keep living it all again. I've always been superstitious.
3 'Cause All I wanted.

The great hunter stepping out of the wind. A savage brother out of the riverbed. I'm still your brother. I'll bet another. What are you doing out of my head? I'm a sinner. A better lover.

I'm on my own instead.
4 The songs are giving back tonight. But I'm lifted like a bird in flight. I'm finding passage in the spite. Said I'm looking for a fight.

Fig. 3 The Battle of Issus, Mosaic, Pompeii ruins

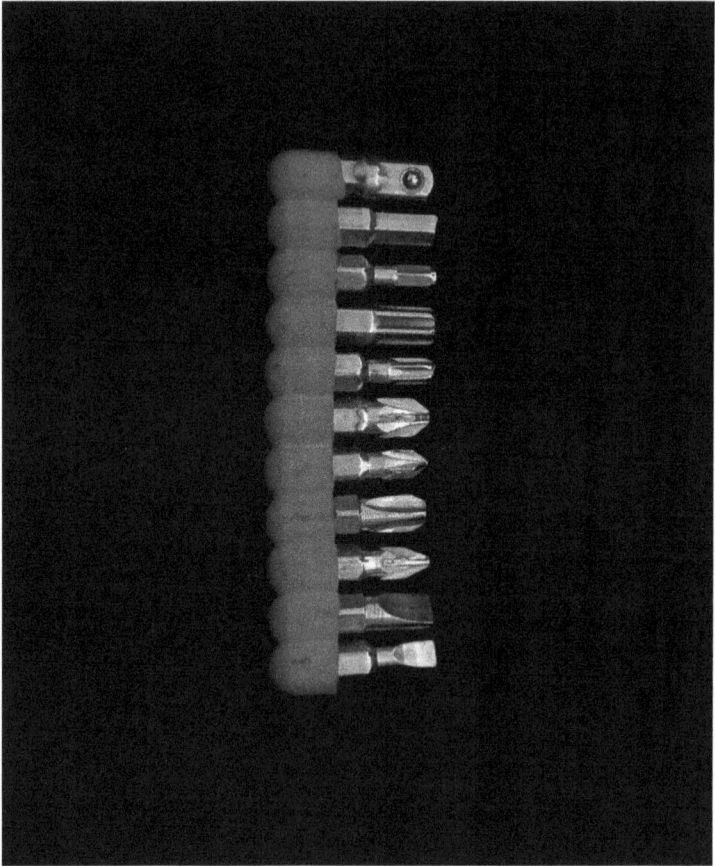

Fig. 4 Driver bits

5 I keep chasing a brand new friend. Sometimes it pays to be driven. We're just tying up old loose ends. You gotta pay to make a livin'. **6** But all I wanted. The great hunter out of the wind. A savage mother content to see me dead. I'll bet another. A better brother. What are you doing out of my bed? But still another. A better color. I'm on my own instead.

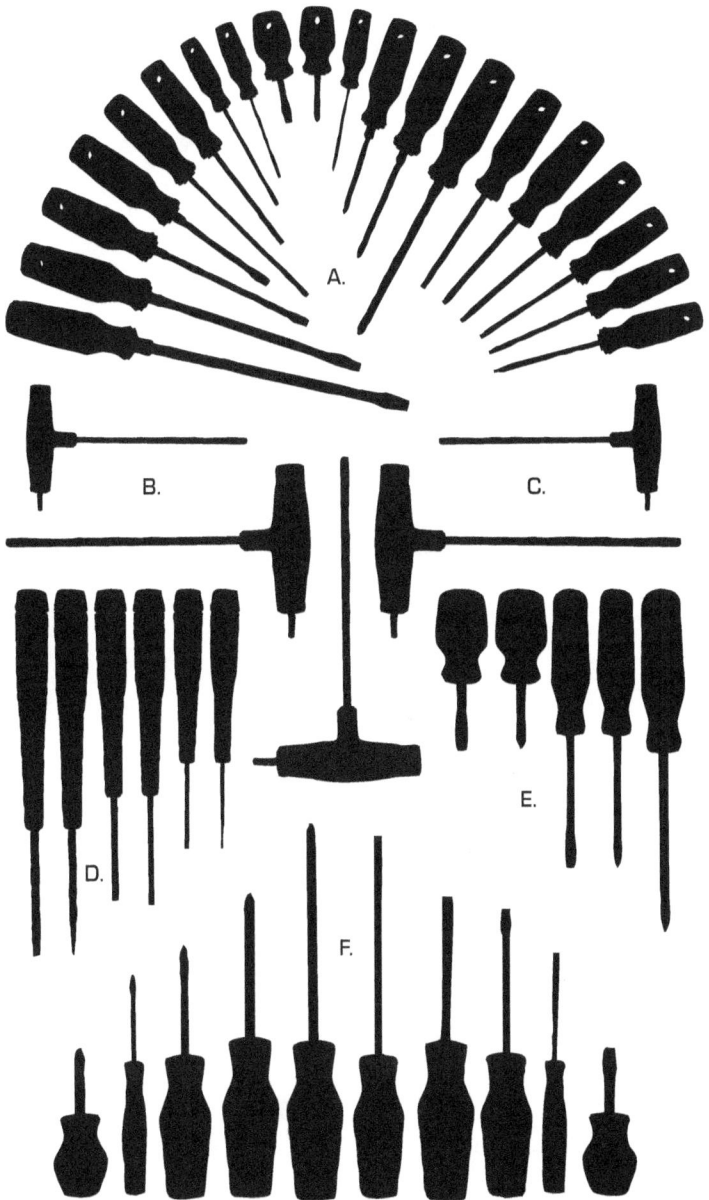

Fig. 5 Screwdrivers

Fig. 6 Transvaal Daisy (gerbera jamesonii)

Fig. 7 Cain and Abel by Orazio Riminaldi, 17th century

7 The songs are giving back tonight. But I'm lifted like a bird in flight. I'm finding passage in the spite. Said I'm looking for a fight.

8 I'm in the wind. I'm living for the fight.

9 I'm in the wind.

10
BUTCHER'S BILL

(6:29)

Fig. 1 Harvest moon

Fig. 2   Moon detail

Butcher's Bill

1 The love seen has passed away. And into dark from which it cannot stray.
2 Our river runs but seldom does it slow. Streams may reverse.

Who knows which way they'll go?
3 The harvest moon will have its say.
4 Oh I can't fight this tide any longer. Or I might drift away in the roll-

ing sea. We're storms of wrathful age growing stronger. Oh won't you hear my words? Come and shelter me.

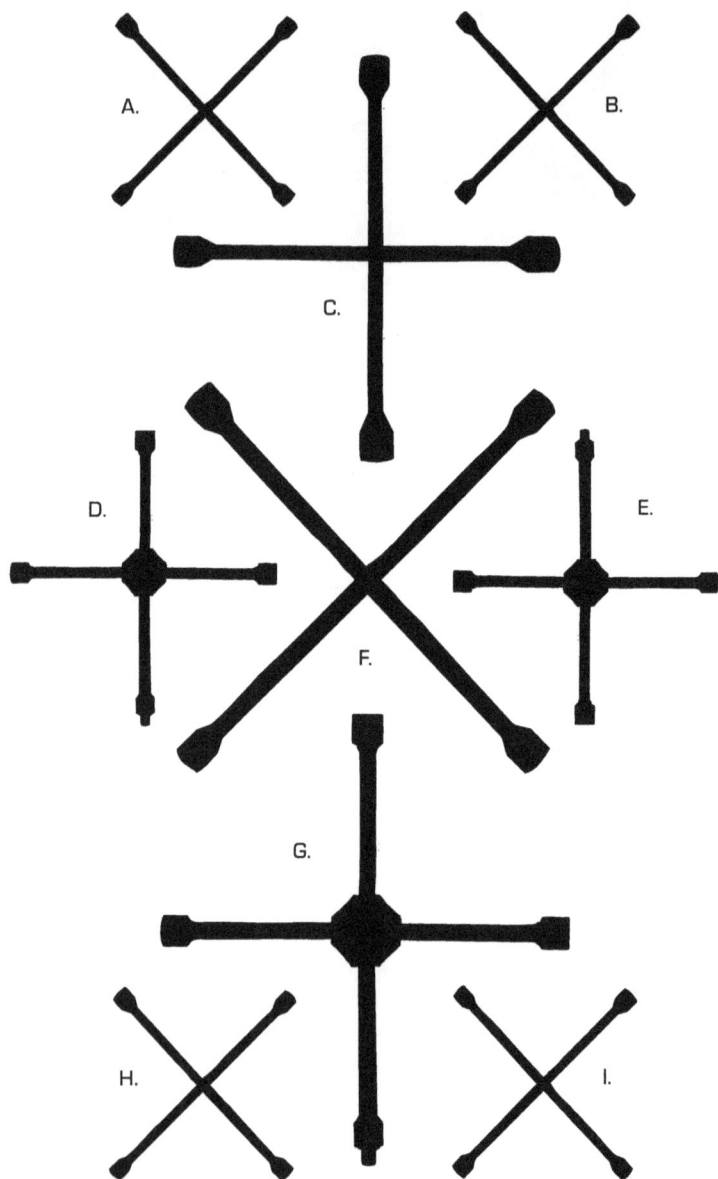

Fig. 3 Lug Wrenches

Fig. 4 Admiral Horatio Nelson (British Navy 18th century)

Fig. 5   We drifted out as younger men

Fig. 6 Tidal wave

5 I grow more tired day by day. My youthful joy has passed away. Each time that I must bare my soul. Each time I dig it takes its toll. Silence meets silence when all hearts are closed. Four hearts to be hearts all must be exposed. **6** With bitter hearts and jealous eyes and aged hands. We say goodbye. **7** We drifted out as younger men. As lesser lights that play upon the sea. I think about it now and then. The lights that call me back to harmony.

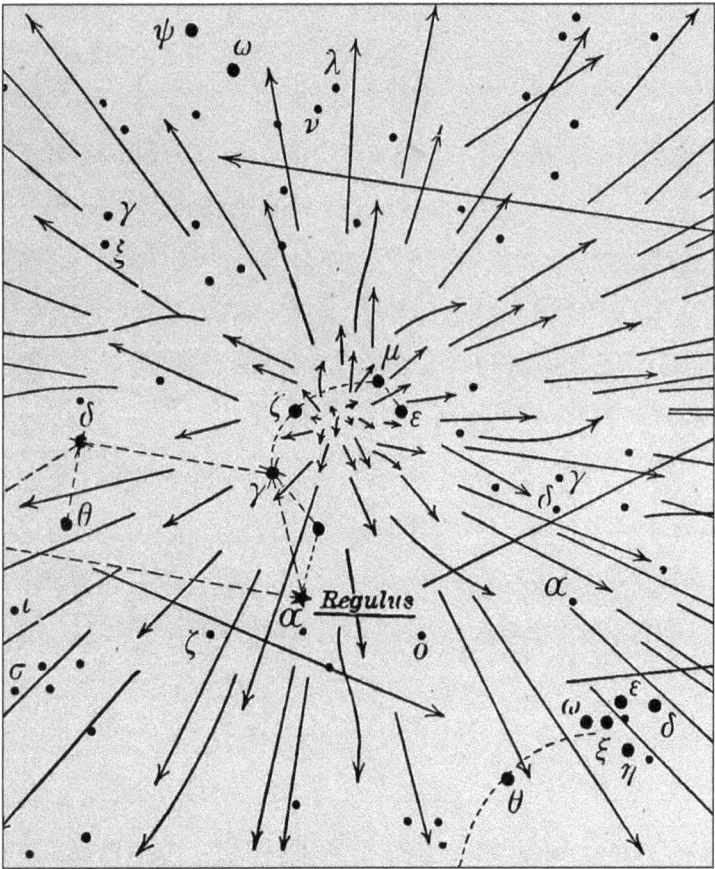

Fig. 7   You found me I was swept away

7 You found me I was swept away. You saved me I was bleeding on the shore. A stranger and a hand in the moonlight.

8 But I can't fight this tide any longer. For I might drift away in the rolling sea. We're storms of wrathful age growing stronger. Oh won't you hear my words? Come and shelter me.

9 Our river runs but seldom does it slow.

10 Our love seen has passed away. And into dark from which it cannot stray. Our river runs but seldom does it slow. Streams may reverse. Who knows which way they'll go?

11 The harvest moon will have its say.

Fig. 8 Ghost orchid (dendropphylax lindenii)

11

THE LAW AND THE SWARM

(3:48)

Fig. 1   Bust of Hammurabi

Fig. 2   Code of Hammurabi

The Law and the Swarm

1 They call me The Law. And I lie to everyone.

2 I'm shielded by the night. I'm blinded by the light. I play the winning hand. And the mask betrays you too.

3 Always start another fight. I tip the winning hand. The mask you wear for you.

4 I'm shielded by the night. I'm blinded by the light. I play the winning hand. And the mask betrays you too.

5 They call me The Swarm. And I can't spare anyone.

Fig. 3   And the mask you wear is you

6 Always out of spite. You keep acting like you might. Tip the winning hand. And the mask who laughs at you.

7 Never understand the plight. Keep it in your hand. And the mask you wear is you.

8 They call me The Law when I lie to everyone. They call me The Swarm and I don't spare anyone.

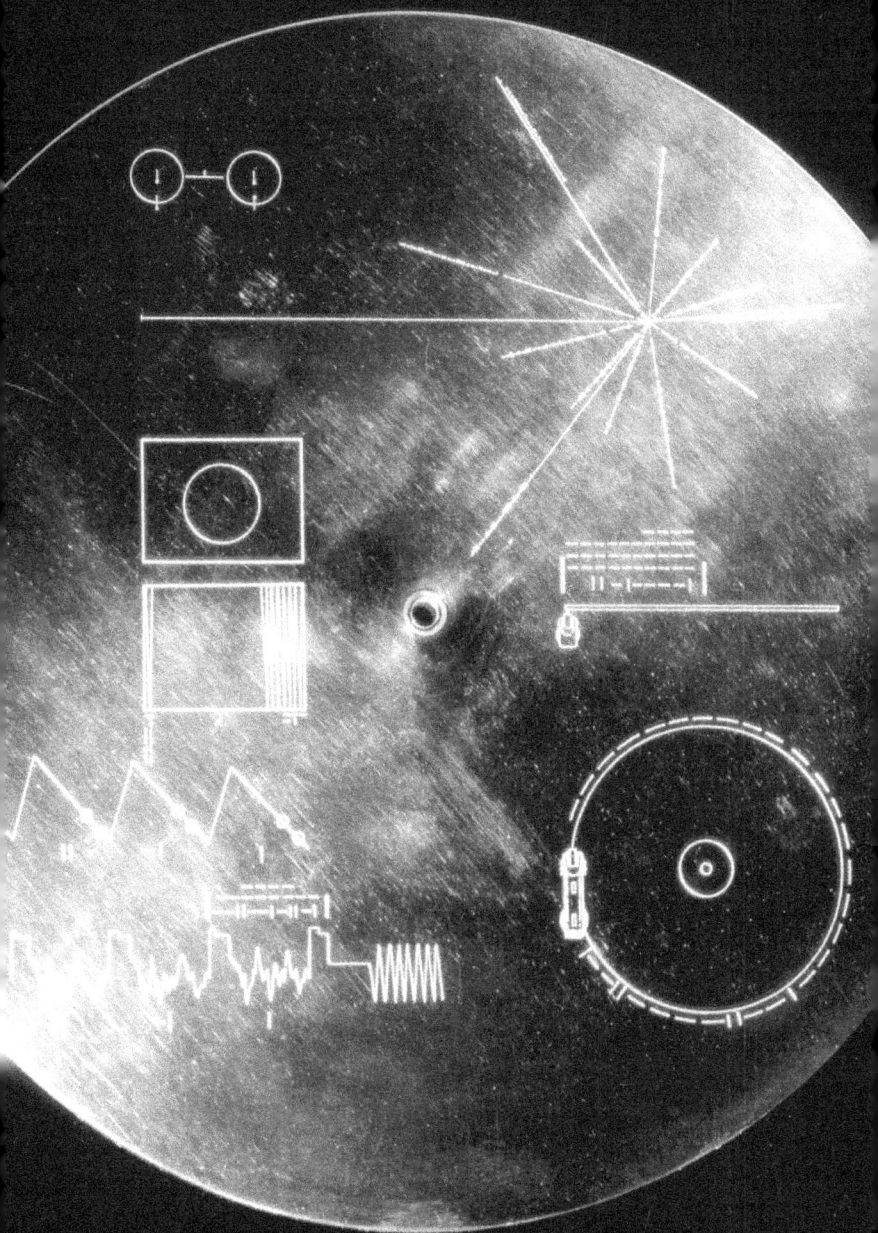

Fig. 4   Voyager golden record

Fig. 5 The march of women

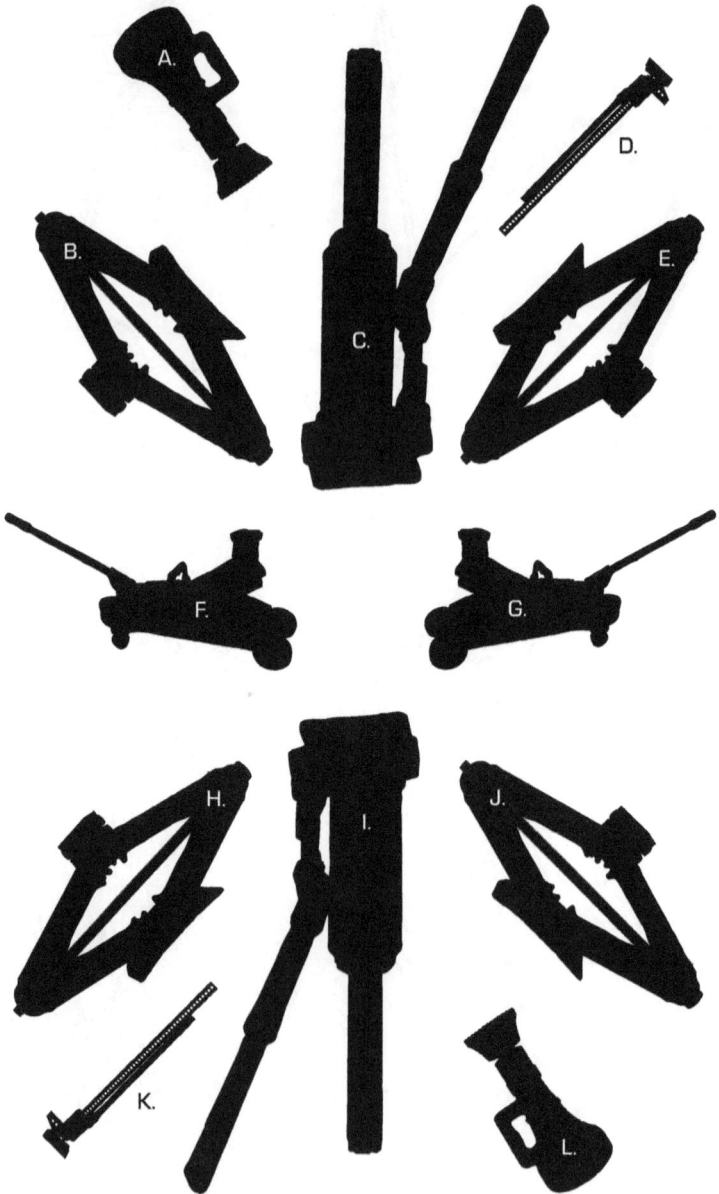

Fig. 6 Tire Jacks

Fig. 7 Ghost orchid (dendropphylax lindenii)

☐ **DESCENDER by Descender** (ALR 001)
6 song debut EP. Available formats: Digipak CD, digital / streaming
90's Influenced post-hardcore. RIYL: Snapcase, Helmet, Quicksand
"Angularly aggressive hardcore that takes an abrasive shape on purpose." – CMJ

☐ **AND SO WE MARCHED by Descender** (ALR 002)
4 song EP. Available formats: Printed book, digital / streaming
90's Influenced post-hardcore. RIYL: Snapcase, Helmet, Quicksand
"...a 21st Century compliant post-hardcore band that was raised on metal and got dosed with a tab of AmRep..."– Jaded Scenster

☐ **TAKING DRUGS TO MAKE MUSIC TO SELL CARS TO by Human Highlight Reel** (ALR 003)
4 song debut EP. Available formats: Vinyl record, printed book, digital / streaming
Instrumental post-rock. RIYL: Maserati, June of 44, Russian Circles
"Aces instrumental post rock. Think Russian Circles or perhaps a more metal Seam..." – Jaded Scenster

☐ **JUDGE by Vagina Panther** (ALR 004)
5 song EP. Available formats: Printed book, digital / streaming
Heavy female-fronted garage rock. RIYL: QOTSA, Cheeseburger, Fu Manchu, Stooges
"Vagina Panther rocks." – Billboard

☐ **BLACK BLACK BLACK by Black Black Black** (ALR 005)
12 song debut LP. Available formats: Vinyl record, printed book, digital / streaming
Melodic death rock. RIYL: Akimbo, Torche, Lungfish, Black Flag
"Brooklyn-by-way-of-Ohio doomsters offer up a big, nasty salute to gas tanks and goat hooves. It all coalesces to form one ravaging feast of melodic death rock that will satiate all your salacious needs, be it Nether-deity worshiping or rock star living." – Broken Beard

☐ **GODMAKER by Godmaker** (ALR 007)
4 song debut LP. Available formats: Vinyl record, printed book, digital / streaming
Doomy sludge metal. RIYL: High on Fire, Red Fang, Mastodon, The Sword
"An example of genuine out of-nowhere brilliance. A patient drawn out campaign of aggression." – Relix

☐ **THE SPACE MERCHANTS by The Space Merchants** (ALR 008)
8 song debut LP. Available formats: Printed book, digital / streaming
Whiskey-soaked space-rock. RIYL: Black Mountain, Dead Meadow, The Besnard Lakes
"A unique brand of lo-fi psych rock... their huge-yet-minimal sound, mixing psych with blues and country style riffs to make something great." – Magnet

☐ **HIRAM-MAXIM by Hiram-Maxim** (ALR 009)
4 song debut LP. Available formats: Vinyl record, printed book, digital / streaming
Noisy experimental doomgaze. RIYL: Swans, Suicide, Pink Floyd, Oxbow
"Builds into an apocalyptic fervor before dissipating into a cloudy haze & ending before you've had your fill." – VICE

☐ **ALTERED STATES OF DEATH AND GRACE by Black Black Black** (ALR 010)
10 song sophomore LP. Available formats: Vinyl record, printed book, digital / streaming
Melodic death rock. RIYL: Akimbo, Torche, Lungfish, Black Flag
"...the kind of good-natured misanthropy of bands like Whores or KEN mode, but the musical gestures beneath the noisy exterior are all forward-charging, Kyuss-worshipping sludge n' roll. It's basically underground metal's version of a radio banger." – BrooklynVegan

☐ **TRESPASSES by Nathaniel Shannon & The Vanishing Twin** (ALR 011)
15 song debut LP. Available formats: Printed book, digital / streaming
Unsettling bedroom recording darkness. RIYL: Lanegan, Badalemnti, Springsteen, Waits
"An unsettling yet captivating collection of songs compiled from a decade of bedroom recordings... Shannon's spoken word-style vocals over haunting and minimalist instrumentals lend a creepy atmosphere to the record." – Decibel

ALSO AVAILABLE FROM AQUALAMB ARTISTS

☐ **FERA by Husbandry** (ALR 012)
8 song debut LP. Available formats: Printed book, CD, digital / streaming
Female-fronted math rock meets post-hardcore. RIYL: Mars Volta, Glassjaw, Refused, Deftones
"It's hard to believe that Husbandry is not the biggest band in the world. They're heavy and mathy, chaos wrapped in hard rock and heavy metal." – Nerdist

☐ **MURDEREDMAN by MURDEREDMAN** (ALR 013)
8 song sophomore LP. Available formats: Vinyl record, printed book, digital / streaming
Post-punk inspired noise rock. RIYL: Savages, Bauhaus, Boris, Killing Joke
"A patient and disciplined examination of anxiety and melancholy underpinned with a cathartic tension-and-release structure that borrows from goth, post-metal, and no-wave..." – New Noise Magazine

☐ **IN TENSIONS by Lo-Pan** (ALR 014)
5 song EP. Available formats: Vinyl record, printed book, CD, digital / streaming
Anthemic desert rock. RIYL: Soundgarden, ASG, Torche, Red Fang
"Calling Lo-Pan a stoner band is a disservice to the amalgam of influences the band successfully merges together: the soulful alt rock of the 90s with a thundering doom/sludge sound that's equal parts immediate and timeless." – Nine Circles

☐ **GHOSTS by Hiram-Maxim** (ALR 015)
7 song LP. Available formats: Vinyl record, printed book, digital / streaming
Noisy experimental doomgaze. RIYL: Swans, Suicide, Pink Floyd, Oxbow
"Everything is awash in mesmerizing ambient skree and squalls of atonal feedback. Think an extended, updated version of side 2 of Black Flag's My War." – Hellride Music

☐ **KISS THE DIRT by The Space Merchants** (ALR 016)
10 song sophomore LP. Available formats: Vinyl record, printed book, digital / streaming
Whiskey-soaked space-rock. RIYL: Black Mountain, Dead Meadow, The Besnard Lakes
"[T]he sonic equivalent of having an acid trip in the bathroom between Woodstock and a ZZ Top concert in '69" – New Noise Magazine

☐ **BAD WEEDS NEVER DIE by Husbandry** (ALR 017)
5 song EP. Available formats: Printed book, CD, digital / streaming
Female-fronted math rock meets post-hardcore. RIYL: Mars Volta, Glassjaw, Refused, Deftones
"While retaining their bold go-anywhere style, the EP is a more streamlined and focused effort, signaling a greater maturity and command of recording." – Echoes and Dust

☐ **BY THE GRACE OF BLOOD AND GUTS by Haan** (ALR 018)
8 song LP. Available formats: Printed book, Vinyl, CD, digital / streaming
Noise, Grime, Sludge, Metal, Rock. RIYL: Unsane, Melvins, Swans, Helmet, Clutch
"If Melvins and Unsane had a kid while under the influence of hallucinogens" – Metal Insider

☐ **LUMINOUS VOLUMES by Skryptor** (ALR 019)
7 song LP. Available formats: Vinyl, Printed book, CD, digital / streaming
Noise, Math rock, Prog. RIYL: craw, Dazzling Killmen, Don Cabellero
"Galloping, off-kilter and unabashedly victorious, proggy noise-rock outfit Skryptor's takes hard-rock/psychedelic throwback tropes, flips them on their heads and stretches it all into an adventurous march through endlessly shifting soundscapes."" – Revolver

☐ **DEAD INSIDE by Frayle** (ALR 021)
7 song 7". Alchemy Box: Printed book, Vinyl, CD, digital / streaming
Heavy witch doom. RIYL: Chelsea Wolfe, Portis Head, Sleep, Sunn O)))
"Trades in dark psychedelics and heavy, dripping drums that punctuate the riffing that plays in and around vocalist Gywn Strang's superb voice." – Nine Circles

☐ **SUBTLE by Lo-Pan** (ALR 022)
11 song LP. Available formats: Vinyl, Printed book, CD, digital / streaming
Anthemic desert rock. RIYL: Soundgarden, ASG, Torche, Red Fang
Subtle was produced by James Brown (NIN, Foo Fighters, Ghost) and mastered by Ted Jensen (Mastodon, Deftones, Bad Company, GNR).

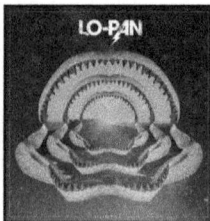

The music for *Subtle*
can be downloaded
via the link below:

http://aqualamb.org/022

www.ingramcontent.com/pod-product-compliance
Lightning Source LLC
Chambersburg PA
CBHW020939090426
42736CB00010B/1192